LET'S FIND
SCREWS

by Wiley Blevins

A SCREW DOES A LOT OF WORK!

A screw holds things together. It helps us to lift things. A screw also makes it easier for us to move things around. A screw is a simple machine.

Do you want to see what a screw is all about? Let's turn the page and find out.

SCREWS TWIST AND SPIN.

The lid on a jar is a screw. How do you keep the food in the jar fresh?

SCREW THE LID ON TIGHT!

5

TURN THE SCREWDRIVER.

Spin, spin. Twist the screw until it's tight.

You **NEED** IT TO HOLD THE PIECES TOGETHER JUST RIGHT.

BUMP, BUMP, BUMP.

Bolts are screws.
They keep the wheels
on the wagon.

UP AND DOWN,
BOLTS
KEEP THE WHEELS ON
SAFE AND SOUND.

A FENCE KEEPS A DOG SAFE IN THE GARDEN.

What does it take to build a tall fence?

LOTS OF WOOD AND LOTS OF SCREWS!

A SCREW MAKES A HOLE IN THE ICE.

It might be hard. It might be thick. But a great big screw drills through . . .

NOW THAT'S THE TRICK!

LOOK CLOSELY AT A SCREW!

The screw looks like a tiny slide wrapped around a pole. What if we unwrap the curving slide?

It would STRETCH OUT LIKE A LONG, SMOOTH RAMP, OR INCLINED PLANE.

PEOPLE CLIMB UP.
PEOPLE CLIMB DOWN.

A staircase is an inclined plane, or ramp. It goes from a higher place to a lower place.

THIS RAMP CURVES AROUND LIKE A GIANT SCREW.

WHOOSH!

This water slide twists around like a screw.

It SPINS THE WATER AROUND, AND YOU TOO!

PUT IN A COIN! TURN THE LEVER!

A little container rolls down the twisty ramp.

WHAT KIND OF TOY WILL YOU FIND INSIDE?

THE CAP TWISTS OFF.
THE CAP TWISTS ON.

A toothpaste tube uses a screw. The cap keeps the toothpaste in.

YOU DON'T WANT IT TO SQUEEZE OUT ALL OVER THE PLACE.

SEE THE SCREW ON THE LIGHT BULB?

It fits into a light just like a lid fits on a jar. Turn the bulb until it's tight. Then switch on the light.

NICE AND BRIGHT!

TWIST THE TOP OFF.

Have a drink if you like. Twist the top on and nothing will spill. A bottle cap is a little lid.

AND IT'S A TINY SCREW.

A TAP IS A SCREW.

Twist one way! Water flows out. Now twist the other way! Keep the water in.

THANKS TO THE SCREW, YOU WON'T WASTE A DROP!

slide

jar lid

tap

bolt

toy vending machine

water slide

screw

bottle top

light bulb

ice drill

staircase

toothpaste cap

Raintree is an imprint of Capstone Global Library Limited, a company incorporated in England and Wales having its registered office at 264 Banbury Road, Oxford, OX2 7DY – Registered company number: 6695582

www.raintree.co.uk
myorders@raintree.co.uk
Copyright © Capstone Global Library Limited 2022

ISBN 978 1 3982 0503 1 (hardback)
ISBN 978 1 3982 0504 8 (paperback)

Edited by Erika Shores
Designed by Kyle Grenz
Media Researcher: Tracy Cummins
Production by Spencer Rosio
Originated by Capstone Global Library Ltd
Printed and bound in India

Image Credits
iStockphoto: choicegraphx, 26–27, YinYang, 4–5; Shutterstock: Adam Gryko, 14–15, ANTONIO TRUZZI, 31 bottom left, Belish, 31 top right, Bildagentur Zoonar GmbH, 6–7, Ekaterina43, 31 bottom right, Erickson Stock, 8–9, gmstockstudio, 30 bottom left, Jan phanomphrai, 28–29, Jason Finn, 30 top left, Johan_Sky, 31 top left, Jr images, 30 middle left, Juliane Franke, 16–17, mapichai, 30 middle right, megastocker, Cover, Michal Bellan, 10–11, MrVander, Design Element, nik93737, 22–23, Somprasong Wittayanupakorn, 2–3, Stephen Mcsweenyllan, 12–13, Stocksnapper, 31 middle right, Sucharas Wongpeth, 30 bottom right, Tii more, 31 middle left, Try my best, 24–25, v74, 20–21, Volodymyr Nikolaiev, 30 top right, yelantsevv, 18–19

British Library Cataloguing in Publication Data
A full catalogue record for this book is available from the British Library.

FIND OUT MORE ABOUT SIMPLE MACHINES BY CHECKING OUT THE WHOLE SERIES!

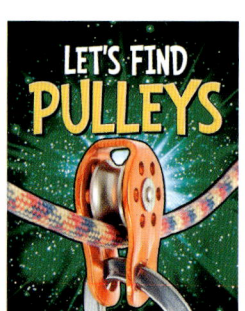

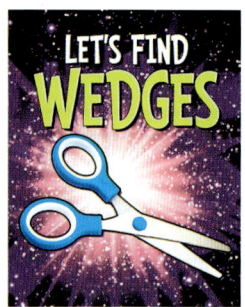

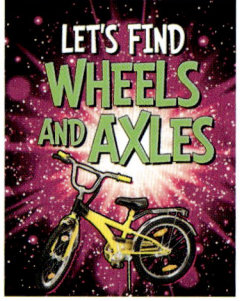

screw

bottle top

light bulb

ice drill

staircase

toothpaste cap

Raintree is an imprint of Capstone Global Library Limited, a company incorporated in England and Wales having its registered office at 264 Banbury Road, Oxford, OX2 7DY – Registered company number: 6695582

www.raintree.co.uk
myorders@raintree.co.uk

ISBN 978 1 3982 0503 1 (hardback)
ISBN 978 1 3982 0504 8 (paperback)

Edited by Erika Shores
Designed by Kyle Grenz
Media Researcher: Tracy Cummins
Production by Spencer Rosio
Originated by Capstone Global Library Ltd
Printed and bound in India

Image Credits
iStockphoto: choicegraphx, 26–27, YinYang, 4–5; Shutterstock: Adam Gryko, 14–15, ANTONIO TRUZZI, 31 bottom left, Belish, 31 top right, Bildagentur Zoonar GmbH, 6–7, Ekaterina43, 31 bottom right, Erickson Stock, 8–9, gmstockstudio, 30 bottom left, Jan phanomphrai, 28–29, Jason Finn, 30 top left, Johan_Sky, 31 top left, Jr images, 30 middle left, Juliane Franke, 16–17, mapichai, 30 middle right, megastocker, Cover, Michal Bellan, 10–11, MrVander, Design Element, nik93737, 22–23, Somprasong Wittayanupakorn, 2–3, Stephen Mcsweenyllan, 12–13, Stocksnapper, 31 middle right, Sucharas Wongpeth, 30 bottom right, Tii more, 31 middle left, Try my best, 24–25, v74, 20–21, Volodymyr Nikolaiev, 30 top right, yelantsevv, 18–19

British Library Cataloguing in Publication Data
A full catalogue record for this book is available from the British Library.

FIND OUT MORE ABOUT SIMPLE MACHINES BY CHECKING OUT THE WHOLE SERIES!

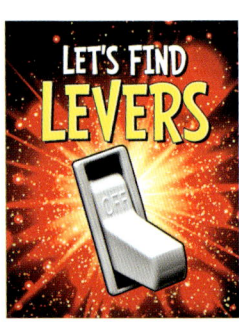

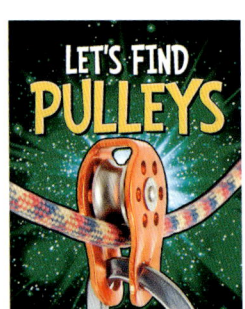

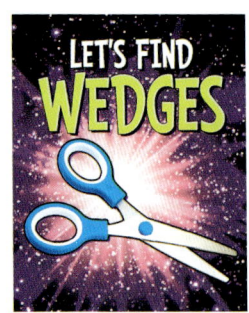

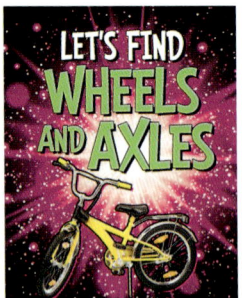